ALL MIXED UP

By Anne Morgan

Illustrated by Tim Haggerty

Sadlier-Oxford
A Division of William H. Sadlier, Inc.
New York, NY 10005-1002

What if things got all mixed up?
You'd be big, and your dad
would be little.

What if things got all mixed up?
You'd take your goldfish for
a walk.

What if things got all mixed up? You'd eat dinner when the sun came up.

What if things got all mixed up?
You'd see pink cows and
pigs with spots.

What if things got all mixed up?
You'd sit up in bed to go to sleep.

What if things got all mixed up?
You'd ride in a ship to get to
school.

What if things really did
get all mixed up?
You'd wish they weren't!